The CopyWorkBook

Comedies of William Shakespeare

BLUE SKY
DAISIES

Images from the Folger Shakespeare Library used under Creative Commons (CC BY-SA 4.0) license; https://luna.folger.edu/luna/servlet

Play title illustrations: Shaw, Byam, 1872-1919, From the Folger Shakespeare Library used un Creative Commons (CC BY-SA 4.0) license: https://luna.folger.edu/luna/servlet

Cover art: Wright, John Massey, 1777-1866, "Illustrations to Shakespeare"

From the Folger Shakespeare Library used under Creative Commons (CC BY-SA 4.0) license: https://luna.folger.edu/luna/servlet

Published by Blue Sky Daisies

Wichita, Kansas

blueskydaisies.wordpress.com

ISBN-13: 978-1-944435-06-6

ISBN-10: 1-944435-06-9

Copywork

Copywork is useful on two fronts: first, the student has practice in developing the skill of carefully and accurately copying sentences and faithfully and neatly reproducing them; second, the student has the opportunity to set his or her mind upon excellent language and meaning.

We think you will enjoy this collection of lines from Shakespeare's comedy plays. You may want to work through the copywork book in order, or you may want to use the pages for the play that you are presently reading. Feel free to jump around and approach the copywork however you prefer.

The Editors
Blue Sky Daisies

The
Comedies

Contents

Introduction

This collection of quotations from William Shakespeare's comedy plays includes well-known epigrams ("Some are born great, some achieve greatness and some have greatness thrust upon 'em") as well as longer excerpts from monologues or soliloquies ("All the world's a stage, / And all the men and women merely players..."). The selections are arranged by comedy play, alphabetically.

Copying the words of Shakespeare trains the ear for the melody of beautiful English, the mind for the contemplation of reasoned rhetoric, and the heart for the language of love—to say nothing of the soul for wit.

From the First Folio, 1623

> The man that hath no music in himself,
> Nor is not moved with concord of sweet sounds,
> Is fit for treasons, stratagems, and spoils.
> The motions of his spirit are dull as night,
> And his affections dark as Erebus.
> Let no such man be trusted. Mark the music.[1]

---

[1]   Merchant of Venice, Act 5, Scene 1, see page 74.

Lafew
Moderate lamentation is the right of the dead, excessive grief the enemy to the living.
(Act 1, Scene 1)

_____

_____

_____

_____

Countess
Love all, trust a few, do wrong to none.
(Act 1, Scene 1)

_____

_____

_____

_____

Helen
'T were all one
That I should love a bright particular star
And think to wed it, he is so above me.
(Act 1, Scene 1)

_____

_____

_____

_____

All's Well That Ends Well

Helen
The wars have so kept you under that you must needs be born under Mars.
(Act 1, Scene 1)

_____

_____

_____

Parolles
Farewell: when thou
hast leisure, say thy prayers; when thou hast none,

_____

_____

_____

remember thy friends: get thee a good husband,
and use him as he uses thee. So, farewell.
(Act 1, Scene 1)

_____

_____

_____

All's Well That Ends Well

Bertram
His good remembrance, sir,
Lies richer in your thoughts than on his tomb.
(Act 1, Scene 2)

_____

_____

_____

_____

Lavatch
Service is no heritage.
(Act 1, Scene 3)

_____

_____

_____

_____

Lavatch
If men could be contented to be what they are, there were no fear in marriage.
(Act 1, Scene 3)

_____

_____

_____

_____

All's Well That Ends Well

Countess
Even so it was with me when I was young.
If we are nature's, these are ours. This thorn
Doth to our rose of youth rightly belong.

_____

_____

_____

_____

Our blood to us, this to our blood is born:
It is the show and seal of nature's truth,
Where love's strong passion is impressed in youth.

_____

_____

_____

_____

By our remembrances of days foregone,
Such were our faults, or then we thought them none.
(Act 1, Scene 3)

_____

_____

_____

_____

All's Well That Ends Well

Helen
Great floods have flown
From simple sources, and great seas have dried
When miracles have by the great'st been denied.
(Act 2, Scene 1)

_____

_____

_____

_____

Parolles
A young man married is a man that's marred.
(Act 2, Scene 3)

_____

_____

_____

_____

Mariana
No legacy is so rich as honesty.
(Act 3, Scene 5)

_____

_____

_____

_____

All's Well That Ends Well

First Lord
The web of our life is of a mingled yarn, good and ill together.
(Act 4, Scene 3)

_____

_____

_____

_____

Helen
All's well that ends well, still the fine's the crown;
Whate'er the course, the end is the renown.
(Act 4, Scene 4)

_____

_____

_____

_____

King
For we are old, and on our quick'st decrees
The inaudible and noiseless foot of Time
Steals ere we can effect them.
(Act 5, Scene 3)

_____

_____

_____

_____

All's Well That Ends Well

William Shakespeare

ACT I SCENE I

Celia
Well said: that was laid on with a trowel.
(Act 1, Scene 2)

_____

_____

_____

_____

Orlando
Thus must I from the smoke into the smother;
From tyrant duke unto a tyrant brother.
(Act 1, Scene 2)

_____

_____

_____

_____

Rosalind
O, how full of briers is this working-day world!
(Act 1, Scene 3)

_____

_____

_____

_____

Rosalind
Beauty provoketh thieves sooner than gold.
(Act 1, Scene 3)

_____

_____

_____

_____

Celia
I like this place and willingly could waste my time in it.
(Act 2, Scene 4)

_____

_____

_____

_____

Adam
Therefore my age is as a lusty winter,
Frosty, but kindly.
(Act 2, Scene 3)

_____

_____

_____

_____

Silvius
In thy youth thou wast as true a lover
As ever sighed upon a midnight pillow.
(Act 2, Scene 4)

_____

_____

_____

_____

Touchstone
We that are true lovers run into strange capers; but as all is mortal in nature, so is all
    nature in love mortal in folly.
(Act 2, Scene 4)

_____

_____

_____

_____

Rosalind
Thou speakest wiser than thou art ware of.
(Act 2, Scene 4)

_____

_____

_____

_____

As You Like It

"Under the Greenwood Tree" is a famous song from As You Like It. This longer passage continues on the facing page.

Amiens
Under the greenwood tree
Who loves to lie with me,
And turn his merry note
Unto the sweet bird's throat,
Come hither, come hither, come hither:
Here shall he see No enemy
But winter and rough weather.

As You Like It

Jaques
Who doth ambition shun

All together here
And loves to live i' th' sun,
Seeking the food he eats
And pleased with what he gets,
Come hither, come hither, come hither:
Here shall he see No enemy
But winter and rough weather.
(Act 2, Scene 5)

Draw your "Under the Greenwood Tree" illustration here.

Jaques
I met a fool i' the forest,
A motley fool.
(Act 2, Scene 7)

_____

_____

_____

_____

Jaques
And thereby hangs a tale.
(Act 2, Scene 7)

_____

_____

_____

_____

Amiens
Blow, blow, thou winter wind! Thou art not so unkind as man's ingratitude.
(Act 2, Scene 7)

_____

_____

_____

_____

Duke S.
True is it that we have seen better days.
(Act 2, Scene 7)

_____

_____

_____

Rosalind
Do you not know I am a woman? When I think, I must speak.
(Act 3, Scene 2)

_____

_____

_____

Rosalind
Down on your knees,
And thank heaven, fasting, for a good man's love.
(Act 3, Scene 5)

_____

_____

_____

Rosalind
I pray you, do not fall in love with me,
For I am falser than vows made in wine.
(Act 3, Scene 5)

_____

_____

_____

_____

Rosalind
Why then, can one desire too much of a good thing?
(Act 4, Scene 1)

_____

_____

_____

_____

Orlando
For ever and a day.
(Act 4, Scene 1)

_____

_____

_____

_____

As You Like It

Rosalind
No, no, Orlando; men are April when they woo, December when they wed: maids
are May when they are maids, but the sky changes when they are wives.
(Act 4, Scene 1)

_____

_____

_____

Touchstone
The fool doth think he is wise, but the wise man knows himself to be a fool.
(Act 5, Scene 1)

_____

_____

_____

Orlando
How bitter a thing it is to look into happiness through another man's eyes!
(Act 5, Scene 2)

_____

_____

_____

_____

As You Like It

Duke Senior
Thou seest we are not all alone unhappy:
This wide and universal theatre
Presents more woeful pageants than the scene
Wherein we play in.
(Act 2, Scene 7)

Jaques (replying to the Duke Senior)
All the world's a stage,
And all the men and women merely players;
They have their exits and their entrances,
And one man in his time plays many parts,
His acts being seven ages.

Continued on page 34.

"All the world's a stage..."

As You Like It

"At first the infant...."

At first the infant,
Mewling and puking in the nurse's arms.

"Then, the whining school-boy...."

Then, the whining school-boy with his satchel
And shining morning face, creeping like snail
Unwillingly to school.

"Then, the lover...."

And then the lover,
Sighing like furnace, with a woeful ballad
Made to his mistress' eyebrow.

Continued on page 36.

As You Like It

William Shakespeare

"Then, a soldier...."

Then, a soldier,
Full of strange oaths, and bearded like the pard,
Jealous in honour, sudden, and quick in quarrel,
Seeking the bubble reputation
Even in the cannon's mouth.

"Then, the justice...."

And then, the justice,
In fair round belly, with a good capon lined,
With eyes severe, and beard of formal cut,
Full of wise saws, and modern instances,
And so he plays his part.

"The sixth age...."

The sixth age shifts
Into the lean and slippered pantaloon,
With spectacles on nose and pouch on side,
His youthful hose, well saved, a world too wide
For his shrunk shank, and his big manly voice,
Turning again toward childish treble, pipes
And whistles in his sound.

Continued on page 38.

36

As You Like It

"Last scene of all...."

Last scene of all,
That ends this strange eventful history,
Is second childishness and mere oblivion,
Sans teeth, sans eyes, sans taste, sans
  everything.
(Act 2, Scene 7)

* "Sans" is French for "without."

William Shakespeare

As You Like It

William Shakespeare

As You Like It

William Shakespeare

Comedy of Errors

Aegon
Yet this my comfort; when your words are done,
My woes end likewise with the evening sun.
(Act 1, Scene 1)

_____

_____

_____

_____

Antipholus of Syracuse
I to the world am like a drop of water
That in the ocean seeks another drop,

_____

_____

_____

_____

Who, falling there to find his fellow forth—
Unseen, inquisitive—confounds himself.
(Act 1, Scene 2)

_____

_____

_____

_____

Comedy of Errors

Dromio of Syracuse
Every why hath a wherefore.
(Act 2, Scene 2)

_____

_____

_____

_____

Antipholus of Syracuse
Am I in earth, in heaven, or in hell?
Sleeping or waking, mad or well-advised?
Known unto these and to myself disguised?

_____

_____

_____

_____

I'll say as they say, and persever so,
And in this mist at all adventures go.
(Act 2, Scene 2)

_____

_____

_____

_____

Comedy of Errors

Dromio of Ephesus
If the skin were parchment, and the blows you gave were ink,
Your own hand-writing would tell you what I think.
(Act 3, Scene 1)

_____

_____

_____

_____

Balthazar
Small cheer and great welcome makes a merry feast.
(Act 3, Scene 1)

_____

_____

_____

_____

Antipholus of Syracuse
If everyone knows us and we know none,
'Tis time, I think, to trudge, pack and be gone.
(Act 3, Scene 2)

_____

_____

_____

_____

Comedy of Errors

Luciana
That love I begg'd for you, he begg'd of me.
Adriana
With what persuasion did he tempt thy love?

_____

_____

_____

Luciana
With words, that in an honest suit might move:
First, he did praise my beauty; then, my speech.
(Act 4, Scene 2)

_____

_____

_____

Dromio of Syracuse
Marry, he must have a long spoon that must eat with the devil.
(Act 4, Scene 3)

_____

_____

_____

Comedy of Errors

Duke
Why, what an intricate impeach is this!
I think, you all have drank of Circe's cup.
(Act 5, Scene 1)

_____

_____

_____

Antipholus of Ephesus
A hungry lean-faced villain,
A mere anatomy.
(Act 5, Scene 1)

_____

_____

_____

Dromio of Ephesus
And now let's go hand in hand, not one before another.
(Act 5, Scene 1)

_____

_____

_____

William Shakespeare

Comedy of Errors

Love's Labour's Lost

King Ferdinand
Let fame, that all hunt after in their lives,
Live registered upon our brazen tombs,
And then grace us in the disgrace of death
When, spite of cormorant devouring time,
Th'endeavour of this present breath may buy
That honour which shall bate his scythe's keen edge
And make us heirs of all eternity.
(Act 1, Scene 1)

Love's Labour's Lost

King Ferdinand
Therefore, brave conquerors—for so you are,
That war against your own affections,
And the huge army of the world's desires

Our court shall be a little academe,
Still and contemplative in living art.
(Act 1, Scene 1)

_____

_____

_____

_____

_____

_____

_____

_____

_____

_____

_____

_____

Love's Labour's Lost

Biron
Why, all delights are vain; but that most vain
Which, with pain purchas'd, doth inherit pain:
As, painfully to pore upon a book,
To seek the light of truth; while truth the while
Doth falsely blind the eyesight of his look:
Light, seeking light, doth light of light beguile:
So, ere you find where light in darkness lies,
Your light grows dark by losing of your eyes.
(Act 1, Scene 1)

Love's Labour's Lost

Biron
At Christmas I no more desire a rose,
Than wish a snow in May's new-fangled shows;
But like of each thing, that in season grows.
(Act 1, Scene 1)

Armado
Assist me, some extemporal god of rhyme,
for I am sure I shall turn sonnet.
Devise, wit: write, pen,
for I am for whole volumes in folio.
(Act 1, Scene 2)

Love's Labour's Lost

Armado
Love is a familiar; love is a devil. There is no evil angel but love.
(Act 1, Scene 2)

_____

_____

_____

Princess of France
Beauty is bought by judgement of the eye,
Not uttered by base sale of chapmen's tongues.
(Act 2, Scene 1)

_____

_____

_____

Biron
Your wit's too hot, it speeds too fast, 'twill tire.
(Act 2, Scene 1)

_____

_____

_____

Dumaine
I would forget her, but a fever she
Reigns in my blood, and will remembered be.
(Act 4, Scene 3)

_____

_____

_____

Dumaine
Once more I'll read the ode that I have writ.

_____

_____

_____

Biron
Once more I'll mark how love can vary wit.
(Act 4, Scene 3)

_____

_____

_____

Love's Labour's Lost

Dumaine
On a day—alack the day!—
Love, whose month is ever May,
Spied a blossom passing fair
Playing in the wanton air:
Through the velvet leaves the wind,
All unseen, can passage find;
That the lover, sick to death,
Wish himself the heaven's breath.
Air, quoth he, thy cheeks may blow;
Air, would I might triumph so!

Continued on next page.

Love's Labour's Lost

But, alack, my hand is sworn
Ne'er to pluck thee from thy thorn;
Vow, alack, for youth unmeet,
Youth so apt to pluck a sweet!
Do not call it sin in me,
That I am forsworn for thee;
Thou for whom Jove would swear
Juno but an Ethiop were;
And deny himself for Jove,
Turning mortal for thy love.
(Act 4, Scene 3)

Love's Labour's Lost

Biron

For when would you, my lord, or you, or you,
Have found the ground of study's excellence,
Without the beauty of a woman's face
From women's eyes this doctrine I derive:
They are the ground, the books, the academes,
From whence doth spring the true Promethean fire.
(Act 4, Scene 3)

"...beauty of a woman's face..."

Love's Labour's Lost

Biron
But love, first learned in a ladies eyes,
Lives not alone immured in the brain,
But with the motion of all elements
Courses as swift as thought in every power,
And gives to every power a double power,
Above their functions and their offices.
(Act 4, Scene 3)

Love's Labour's Lost

Biron
From women's eyes this doctrine I derive:
They sparkle still the right Promethean fire;
They are the books, the arts, the academes,
That show, contain, and nourish all the world;
Else, none at all in aught proves excellent:
Then fools you were these women to forswear;
Or, keeping what is sworn, you will prove fools.
(Act 4, Scene 3)

Moth
They have been at a great feast of languages, and stolen the scraps.
(Act 5, Scene 1)

_____

_____

_____

_____

Boyet
The tongues of mocking wenches are as keen
As the razor's edge invisible,
Cutting a smaller hair than may be seen;

_____

_____

_____

_____

Above the sense of sense: so sensible
Seemeth their conference; their conceits have wings,
Fleeter than arrows, bullets, wind, thought, swifter things.
(Act 5, Scene 2)

_____

_____

_____

_____

Love's Labour's Lost

Winter Song

When icicles hang by the wall
    And Dick the shepherd blows his nail
And Tom bears logs into the hall
    And milk comes frozen home in pail,
When blood is nipp'd and ways be foul,
Then nightly sings the staring owl,
            Tu-whit;
Tu-who, a merry note,
While greasy Joan doth keel the pot.

Continued on next page.

"Then nightly sings the staring owl..."

63

Love's Labour's Lost

When all aloud the wind doth blow
    And coughing drowns the parson's saw
And birds sit brooding in the snow
    And Marian's nose looks red and raw,
When roasted crabs hiss in the bowl,
Then nightly sings the staring owl,
             Tu-whit;
Tu-who, a merry note,
While greasy Joan doth keel the pot.

Armado
The words of Mercury are harsh after the
songs of Apollo. You, that way; we, this way.
(Act 5, Scene 2)

"And birds sit brooding in the snow..."

Love's Labour's Lost

William Shakespeare

Measure for Measure

Lucio
Our doubts are traitors,
And make us lose the good we oft might win
By fearing to attempt.
(Act 1 Scene 5)

_____

_____

_____

_____

Escalus
Some rise by sin, and some by virtue fall.
(Act 2, Scene 1)

_____

_____

_____

_____

Angelo
Condemn the fault and not the actor of it?
(Act 2, Scene 2)

_____

_____

_____

_____

William Shakespeare

Measure for Measure

Isabella
O, it is excellent
To have a giant's strength, but it is tyrannous
To use it like a giant.
(Act 2, Scene 2)

_____

_____

_____

_____

Angelo
Is this her fault, or mine?
The tempter, or the tempted, who sins most?
(Act 2, Scene 2)

_____

_____

_____

_____

Claudio
The miserable have no other medicine
But only hope.
(Act 3, Scene 1)

_____

_____

_____

_____

Measure for Measure

Duke

The hand that hath made you fair, hath made you good: the goodness, that is cheap
in beauty, makes beauty brief in goodness; but grace, being the soul of your
complexion, should keep the body ever fair.
(Act 3, Scene 1)

Duke

Virtue is bold, and goodness never fearful.
(Act 3, Scene 1)

Duke

Twice treble shame on Angelo,
To weed my vice, and let his grow!
(Act 3, Scene 1)

Measure for Measure

Duke
O, what may man within him hide,
Though angel on the outward side!
(Act 3, Scene 1)

_____

_____

_____

_____

Duke
Haste still pays haste, and leisure answers leisure,
Like doth quit like, and *measure* still for *measure*.
(Act 5, Scene 1)

_____

_____

_____

_____

Duke
What's mine is yours and what is yours is mine.
(Act 5, Scene 1)

_____

_____

_____

_____

Measure for Measure

The Merchant of Venice

Antonio
I hold the world but as the world, Gratiano,
A stage where every man must play a part,
And mine a sad one.
(Act 1, Scene 1)

_____

_____

_____

Portia
God made him, and therefore let him pass for a man.
(Act 1, Scene 2)

_____

_____

_____

Shylock
I will buy with you, sell with you, talk with you, walk with you, and so following; but
    I will not eat with you, drink with you, nor pray with you.
(Act 1, Scene 3)

_____

_____

_____

The Merchant of Venice

Antonio
Mark you this, Bassanio,
The devil can cite Scripture for his purpose.
An evil soul, producing holy witness,

_____

_____

_____

_____

Is like a villain with a smiling cheek;
A goodly apple rotten at the heart;
O, what a goodly outside falshood hath!
(Act 1, Scene 3)

_____

_____

_____

_____

Bassanio
I like not fair terms and a villain's mind.
(Act 1, Scene 3)

_____

_____

_____

_____

The Merchant of Venice

Morocco
Mislike me not for my complexion,
The shadowed livery of the burnished sun.
(Act 2, Scene 1)

_____

_____

_____

_____

Lancelot
It is a wise father that knows his own child.
(Act 2, Scene 2)

_____

_____

_____

_____

Jessica
But love is blind, and lovers cannot see
The pretty follies that themselves commit.
(Act 2, Scene 6)

_____

_____

_____

_____

The Merchant of Venice

Morocco
All that glisters is not gold,
Often have you heard that told:
Many a man his life hath sold,
But my outside to behold:
Gilded tombs do worms infold.
Had you been as wise as bold,
Young in limbs, in judgment old,
Your answer had not been inscrol'd:
Fare you well; your suit is cold.
(Act 2, Scene 7)

Draw Morocco speaking.

The Merchant of Venice

Draw Portia with the three metal boxes.

Morocco
The first, of gold, who this inscription bears,
Who chooseth me, shall gain what many men desire.
The second, silver, which this promise carries;
Who chooseth me, shall get as much as he deserves.
This third, dull lead, with warning all as blunt;
Who chooseth me, must give and hazard all he hath.
How shall I know if I do choose the right?

Portia
The one of them contains my picture, prince;
If you choose that, then I am yours withal.
(Act 2, Scene 7)

The Merchant of Venice

Aragon
The portrait of a blinking idiot.
(Act 2, Scene 9)

_____

_____

_____

Shylock
If you prick us, do we not bleed?
If you tickle us, do we not laugh?

_____

_____

_____

If you poison us, do we not die?
And if you wrong us, shall we not revenge?
(Act 3, Scene 1)

_____

_____

_____

The Merchant of Venice

Singer
Tell me where is fancy bred,
Or in the heart or in the head?
(Act 3, Scene 2)

_____

_____

_____

_____

Duke
I never knew so young a body with so old a head.
(Act 4, Scene 1)

_____

_____

_____

_____

Shylock
The pound of flesh, which I demand of him,
Is dearly bought, is mine, and I will have it:
(Act 4, Scene 1)

_____

_____

_____

_____

The Merchant of Venice

Portia
The quality of mercy is not strained,
It droppeth as the gentle rain from heaven
Upon the place beneath. It is twice blest:
It blesseth him that gives and him that takes.
"Tis mightiest in the mightiest; it becomes
The throned monarch better than his crown:
His scepter shows the force of temporal power,
The attribute to awe and majesty,
Wherein doth sit the dread and fear of kings;

Continued on next page.

The Merchant of Venice

But mercy is above this scepter'd sway,
It is enthroned in the hearts of kings,
It is an attribute to God himself;
And earthly power doth then show likest God's,
When mercy seasons justice. Therefore, Jew,
Though justice be thy plea, consider this,
That, in the course of justice, none of us
Should see salvation: we do pray for mercy;
And that same prayer doth teach us all to render
The deeds of mercy.
(Act 4, Scene 1)

The Merchant of Venice

Portia
Why, this bond is forfeit;
And lawfully by this the Jew may claim
A pound of flesh, to be by him cut off

_____

_____

_____

_____

Nearest the merchant's heart: Be merciful;
Take thrice thy money; bid me tear the bond.
(Act 4, Scene 1)

_____

_____

_____

_____

Portia
Why then, thus it is.
You must prepare your bosom for his knife.
(Act 4, Scene 1)

_____

_____

_____

_____

86

The Merchant of Venice

Portia
This bond doth give thee here no jot of blood;
The words expressly are, a pound of flesh:

_____

_____

_____

_____

Take then thy bond, take thou thy pound of flesh;
But, in the cutting it, if thou dost shed

_____

_____

_____

One drop of Christian blood, thy lands and goods
Are, by the laws of Venice, confiscate
Unto the state of Venice.
(Act 4, Scene 1)

_____

_____

_____

_____

The Merchant of Venice

Illustrate one of the "nights" described.

Illustrate another of the "nights" described.

Lorenzo

The moon shines bright: In such a night as this,
When the sweet wind did gently kiss the trees,
And they did make no noise; in such a might,
Troilus, methinks, mounted the Trojan walls,
And sigh'd his soul towärd the Grecian tents,
Where Cressid lay that night.

Jessica

          In such a night,
Did Thisbe fearfully o'ertrip the dew;
And saw the lion's shadow ere himself,
And ran dismay'd away.

Lorenzo

          In such a night,
Stood Dido with a willow in her hand
Upon the wild sea-banks, and wav'd her love
To come again to Carthage.

Jessica

          In such a night,
Medea gather'd the enchanted herbs
That did renew old Æsom.

Lorenzo

          In such a night,
Did Jessica steal from the wealthy Jew:
And with an unthrift love did run from Venice,
As far as Belmont.

Jessica

          And in such a night,
Did young Lorenzo swear he lov'd her well;
Stealing her soul with many vows of faith,
And ne'er a true one.
(Act 5, Scene 1)

The Merchant of Venice

The Merchant of Venice

Lorenzo
How sweet the moon-light sleeps upon this bank!
Here will we sit, and let the sounds of music
Creep in our ears; soft stillness, and the night,
Become the touches of sweet harmony.
Sit, Jessica: Look, how the floor of heaven
Is thick inlaid with patines of bright gold;
There's not the smallest orb, which thou behold'st,
But in his motion like an angel sings,
Still quiring to the young-ey'd cherubins:
Such harmony is in immortal souls;
But, whilst this muddy vesture of decay
Doth grossly close it in, we cannot hear it.
(Act 5, Scene 1)

The Merchant of Venice

Portia
That light we see, is burning in my hall.
How far that little candle throws his beams!
So shines a good deed in a naughty world.

Nerissa
When the moon shone, we did not see the candle.

Portia
So doth the greater glory dim the less:
A substitute shines brightly as a king,
Until a king be by; and then his state
Empties itself, as doth an inland brook
Into the main of waters.
(Act 5, Scene 1)

Lorenzo
The man that hath no music in himself,
Nor is not moved with concord of sweet sounds,
Is fit for treasons, stratagems and spoils.
The motions of his spirit are dull as night
And his affections dark as Erebus.
Let no such man be trusted.
(Act 5, Scene 1)

The Merchant of Venice

Bassanio
Sweet Portia,
If you did know to whom I gave the ring,
If you did know for whom I gave the ring,
And would conceive for what I gave the ring,
And how unwillingly I left the ring,
When naught would be accepted but the ring,
You would abate the strength of your displeasure.

Portia
If you had known the virtue of the ring,
Or half her worthiness that gave the ring,
Or your own honour to contain the ring,
You would not then have parted with the ring.
(Act 5, Scene 1)

Draw Bassanio and Portia.

The Merchant of Venice

The Merry Wives of Windsor

Slender

All his successors, gone before him, have done 't; and all his ancestors, that come
after him, may.

(Act 1, Scene 1)

_____

_____

_____

_____

Pistol

Thou art the Mars of malcontents.

(Act 1, Scene 3)

_____

_____

_____

_____

Mistress Quickly

Here will be an old abusing of God's patience and the King's English.

(Act 1, Scene 4)

_____

_____

_____

_____

The Merry Wives of Windsor

Nim
I love not the humour of bread and cheese.
(Act 2, Scene 1)

_____

_____

_____

_____

Pistol
Why, then the world's mine oyster, which I with sword will open.
(Act 2, Scene 2)

_____

_____

_____

_____

Mistress Quickly
Marry, this is the short and the long of it.
(Act 2, Scene 2)

_____

_____

_____

_____

The Merry Wives of Windsor

Falstaff
Setting the attraction of my good parts aside, I have no other charms.
(Act 2, Scene 2)

_____

_____

_____

_____

Falstaff
Of what quality was your love then?
Ford
Like a fair house, built upon another man's ground
(Act 2, Scene 2)

_____

_____

_____

_____

Ford
Better three hours too soon than a minute too late.
(Act 2, Scene 2)

_____

_____

_____

_____

The Merry Wives of Windsor

Mistress Page
I cannot tell what the dickens his name is.
(Act 3, Scene 2)

_____

_____

_____

_____

Falstaff
A man of my kidney.
(Act 3, Scene 5)

_____

_____

_____

_____

Falstaff
As good luck would have it.
(Act 3, Scene 5)

_____

_____

_____

_____

The Merry Wives of Windsor

Mistress Page
Why, woman, your husband is in his old lunes again. He so takes on yonder with my husband; so rails against all married mankind; so curses all Eve's daughters, of what complexion soever.
(Act 4, Scene 2)

_____

_____

_____

_____

Mistress Page
Wives may be merry, and yet honest too.
(Act 4, Scene 2)

_____

_____

_____

_____

Falstaff
I hope good luck lies in odd numbers.
(Act 5, Scene 1)

_____

_____

_____

_____

The Merry Wives of Windsor

Falstaff
O powerful love, that in some respects makes a beast a man; in some other, a man a
  beast.
(Act 5, Scene 5)

_____

_____

_____

_____

Falstaff
I think the devil will not have me damned, lest the oil that's in me should set hell on
  fire.
(Act 5, Scene 5)

_____

_____

_____

_____

Ford
In love the heavens themselves do guide the state.
Money buys lands, and wives are sold by fate.
(Act 5, Scene 5)

_____

_____

_____

_____

The Merry Wives of Windsor

William Shakespeare

ACT I SCENE I

A MIDSVMMER
NIGHTS DREAM

A Midsummer Night's Dream

Lysander
The course of true love never did run smooth.
(Act 1, Scene 1)

_____

_____

_____

_____

Helena
Love looks not with the eyes, but with the mind;
And therefore is wing'd Cupid painted blind.
(Act 1, Scene 1)

_____

_____

_____

_____

Fairy
I must go seek some dewdrops here,
And hang a pearl in every cowslip's ear.
(Act 2, Scene 1)

_____

_____

_____

_____

A Midsummer Night's Dream

Oberon
I'll met by moonlight, proud Titania.
(Act 2, Scene 1)

_____

_____

_____

_____

Oberon
I know a bank where the wild thyme blows,
Where oxlips and the nodding violet grows,
Quite over-canopied with luscious woodbine,

_____

_____

_____

_____

With sweet musk-roses and with eglantine:
There sleeps Titania sometime of the night,
Lulled in these flowers with dances and delight.
(Act 2, Scene 1)

_____

_____

_____

_____

Quince
Bless thee, Bottom! Bless thee! Thou art translated.
(Act 3, Scene 1)

———————————————————————————

———————————————————————————

———————————————————————————

———————————————————————————

Titania
What angel wakes me from my flowery bed?
(Act 3, Scene 1)

———————————————————————————

———————————————————————————

———————————————————————————

———————————————————————————

Bottom
And yet, to say the truth, reason and love keep little company together now-a-days
(Act 3, Scene 1)

———————————————————————————

———————————————————————————

———————————————————————————

———————————————————————————

A Midsummer Night's Dream

Puck
I go, I go; look how I go, too
Swifter than arrow from the Tartar's bow.

Oberon
Flower of this purple dye,
Hit with Cupid's archery,
Sink in apple of his eye,
When his love he doth espy,
Let her shine as gloriously
As the Venus of the sky.
When thou wak'st, if she be by,
Beg of her for remedy.

Continued on next page.

"Sink in apple of his eye..."

A Midsummer Night's Dream

Puck
Captain of our fairy band,
Helena is here at hand;
And the youth, mistook by me,
Pleading for a lover's fee.
Shall we their fond pageant see?
Lord, what fools these mortals be!
(Act 3, Scene 2)

"Helena is here at hand..."

A Midsummer Night's Dream

Helena
O, when she's angry, she is keen and shrewd.
She was a vixen when she went to school,
And though she be but little, she is fierce.
(Act 3, Scene 2)

Lysander
Get you gone, you dwarf;
You minimus, of hindering knot-grass made;
You bead, you acorn.
(Act 3, Scene 2)

Puck
Cupid is a knavish lad,
Thus to make poor females mad.
(Act 3, Scene 2)

A Midsummer Night's Dream

Puck
On the ground
Sleep sound:
I'll apply
To your eye,
Gentle lover, remedy.

When thou wakest,
Thou takest
True delight
In the sight
Of thy former lady's eye:

Continued on next page.

Continued on next page.

"I'll apply to your eye..."

A Midsummer Night's Dream

Puck
And the country proverb known,
That every man should take his own,
In your waking shall be shown:
Jack shall have Jill;
Nought shall go ill;
The man shall have his mare again, and all shall be well.
(Act 3, Scene 2)

_____

_____

_____

_____

_____

_____

_____

_____

_____

_____

_____

_____

A Midsummer Night's Dream

Titania
Methought I was enamoured of an ass.
(Act 4, Scene 1)

_____

_____

_____

_____

Bottom
I have had a most rare vision. I had a dream, past the wit of man to say what dream it
    was…

_____

_____

_____

_____

The eye of man hath not heard, the ear of man hath not seen, man's hand is not able
    to taste, his tongue to conceive, nor his heart to report, what my dream was.
(Act 4, Scene 1)

_____

_____

_____

_____

William Shakespeare

A Midsummer Night's Dream

Theseus

More strange than true: I never may believe
These antique fables, nor these fairy toys.
Lovers and madmen have such seething brains,
Such shaping fantasies, that apprehend
More than cool reason ever comprehends.
The lunatic, the lover, and the poet,
Arc of imagination all compact:
One sees more devils than vast hell can hold,
That is, the madman: the lover, all as frantic,
Sees Helen's beauty in a brow of Egypt:
The poet's eye, in a fine frenzy rolling,
Doth glance from heaven to earth, from earth to heaven;
(Act 5, Scene 1)

_____

_____

_____

_____

_____

_____

_____

_____

_____

_____

_____

_____

_____

A Midsummer Night's Dream

Puck

...not a mouse
Shall disturb this hallowed house.
I am sent with broom before,
To sweep the dust behind the door.

Puck

If we shadows have offended,
Think but this, and all is mended,
That you have but slumbered here
While these visions did appear.
(Act 5, Scene 1)

Draw Puck.

A Midsummer Night's Dream

Much Ado About Nothing

Leonato
There's a skirmish of wit between them.
(Act 1, Scene 1)

_____

_____

_____

_____

Don Pedro
In time the savage bull doth bear the yoke.
(Act 1, Scene 1)

_____

_____

_____

_____

Don John
I had rather be a canker in a hedge than a rose in his grace,
(Act 1, Scene 3)

_____

_____

_____

_____

Much Ado About Nothing

Beatrice
He that hath a beard is more than a youth,
and he that hath no beard is less than a man:

_____

_____

_____

_____

and he that is more than a youth is not for me,
and he that is less than a man,
I am not for him.
(Act 2, Scene 1)

_____

_____

_____

_____

Beatrice
As merry as the day is long.
(Act 2, Scene 1)

_____

_____

_____

_____

Much Ado About Nothing

Don Pedro
Speak low if you speak love.
(Act 2, Scene 1)

_____

_____

_____

_____

Claudio
Friendship is constant in all other things,
Save in the office and affairs of love.
(Act 2, Scene 1)

_____

_____

_____

_____

Benedick
She speaks poniards, and every word stabs.
(Act 2, Scene 1)

_____

_____

_____

_____

William Shakespeare

Much Ado About Nothing

Don Pedro
She were an excellent wife for Benedick.

Leonato
O Lord, my lord, if they were but a week
married, they would talk themselves mad.
(Act 2, Scene 1)

Benedick
I will not be sworn, but love may transform me to an oyster.
(Act 2, Scene 3)

Much Ado About Nothing

Benedick

One woman is fair, yet I am well; another is wise, yet I am well; another virtuous, yet I am well; but till all graces be in one woman, one woman shall not come in my grace.

Rich she shall be, that's certain; wise, or I'll none; virtuous, or I'll never cheapen her; fair, or I'll never look on her; mild, or come not near me; noble, or not I for an angel; of good discourse, an excellent musician, and her hair shall be of what colour it please God.

(Act 2, Scene 3)

Much Ado About Nothing

Balthasar
Sigh no more, ladies, sigh no more,
Men were deceivers ever,
One foot in sea and one on shore,
To one thing constant never:
Then sigh not so, but let them go,
And be you blithe and bonny,
Converting all your sounds of woe
Into Hey nonny, nonny.
(Act 2, Scene 3)

How would you illustrate this song? Draw your design below.

William Shakespeare

Much Ado About Nothing

Benedick
When I said I would die a bachelor, I did not think I should live till I were married.
(Act 2, Scene 3)

_____

_____

_____

_____

Hero
Some Cupid kills with arrows, some with traps.
(Act 3, Scene 1)

_____

_____

_____

_____

Benedick
Everyone can master a grief but he that has it.
(Act 3, Scene 2)

_____

_____

_____

_____

Much Ado About Nothing

Dogberry
Are you good men and true?
(Act 3, Scene 3)

_____

_____

_____

_____

Beatrice
I love you with so much of my heart that none is left to protest.
(Act 4, Scene 1)

_____

_____

_____

_____

Leonato
For there was never yet philosopher
That could endure the toothache patiently.
(Act 5, Scene 1)

_____

_____

_____

_____

Much Ado About Nothing

Benedick
In a false quarrel there is no true valour.
(Act 5, Scene 1)

_____

_____

_____

_____

Benedick
Thou and I are too wise to woo peaceably.
(Act 5, Scene 2)

_____

_____

_____

_____

Leonato
Peace! I will stop your mouth.
(Act 5, Scene 3)

_____

_____

_____

_____

Much Ado About Nothing

THE
TAMING OF THE
SHREW

Taming of the Shrew

Christopher Sly
I'll not budge an inch.
(Induction, Scene 1)

_____

_____

_____

_____

Christopher Sly
Come, madam wife, sit by my side,
And let the world slip: we shall ne'er be younger.
(Induction, Scene 2)

_____

_____

_____

_____

Tranio
No profit grows where is no pleasure ta'en:
In brief, sir, study what you most affect.
(Act 1, Scene 1)

_____

_____

_____

_____

Hortensio
There's small choice in rotten apples.
(Act 1, Scene 1)

_____

_____

_____

_____

Tranio
I pray, sir, tell me, is it possible
That love should of a sudden take such hold?
(Act 1, Scene 1)

_____

_____

_____

_____

Petruchio
Such wind as scatters young men through the world
To seek their fortunes further than at home,
Where small experience grows.
(Act 1, Scene 2)

_____

_____

_____

_____

Taming of the Shrew

Petruchio

Say that she rail, why then I'll tell her plain
She sings as sweetly as a nightingale:
Say that she frown, I'll say she looks as clear
As morning roses newly washed with dew:
Say she be mute and will not speak a word,
Then I'll commend her volubility,
And say she uttereth piercing eloquence:
If she do bid me pack, I'll give her thanks,
As though she bid me stay by her a week:
If she deny to wed, I'll crave the day
When I shall ask the banns and when be married.
(Act 2, Scene 1)

* a delicacy or choice food; a dainty

Petruchio
You lie, in faith, for you are called plain Kate,
And bonny Kate and sometimes Kate the curst,
But Kate, the prettiest Kate in Christendom,
Kate of Kate Hall, my super-dainty Kate
For dainties are all cates:* and therefore, Kate,
Take this of me, Kate of my consolation;
Hearing thy mildness prais'd in every town,
Thy virtues spoke of, and thy beauty sounded,
Yet not so deeply as to thee belongs,
Myself am mov'd to woo thee for my wife.
(Act 2, Scene 1)

Draw Kate.

Taming of the Shrew

Katharina
If I be waspish, best beware my sting.

_____

_____

Petruchio
My remedy is, then, to pluck it out.

_____

_____

Katharina
Ay, if the fool could find it where it lies.

_____

_____

Petruchio
Who knows not where a wasp does wear his sting? In his tail.

_____

_____

Katharina
In his tongue.

_____

_____

Petruchio
Whose tongue?

_____

_____

Katharina
Yours, if you talk of tails; and so farewell.
(Act 2, Scene 1)

_____

_____

Bianca
Old fashions please me best; I am not so nice,
To change true rules for old inventions.
(Act 3, Scene 1)

_____

_____

_____

_____

Katharina
Forward, I pray, since we have come so far,
And be it moon, or sun, or what you please.

_____

_____

_____

_____

And if you please to call it a rush-candle,
Henceforth I vow it shall be so for me.
(Act 4, Scene 5)

_____

_____

_____

_____

Taming of the Shrew

Katharina

I am asham'd, that women are so simple
To offer war where they should kneel for peace,
Or seek for rule, supremacy, and sway,
When they are bound to serve, love, and obey.
Why are our bodies soft, and weak, and smooth.
Unapt to toil and trouble in the world,
But that our soft conditions, and offr hearts,
Should well agree with our external parts
Come, come, you froward and unable worms,
My mind hath been as big as one of yours,

Continued on next page.

Taming of the Shrew

Continued from previous page.

My heart as great, my reason, haply, more
To bandy word for word, and frown for frown;
But now I see our lances are but straws,
Our strength as weak, our weakness past compare,
That seeming to be most, which we indeed least are.
Then vail your stomachs, for it is no boot,
And place your hands below your husband's foot:
In token of which duty, if he please,
My hand is ready, may it do him ease.

Petruchio
Why, there's a wench! Come on, and kiss me, Kate.
(Act 5, Scene 2)

Draw Petruchio and Kate.

Taming of the Shrew

William Shakespeare

The Tempest

Gonzalo

Now would I give a thousand furlongs of sea for an acre of barren ground; long
heath, brown furze, any thing. The wills above be done! but I would fain die a
dry death.
(Act 1, Scene 1)

_____

_____

_____

_____

Miranda

If by your art, my dearest father, you have
Put the wild waters in this roar, allay them.
(Act 1, Scene 2)

_____

_____

_____

_____

Prospero

Now I arise,
Sit still, and hear the last of our sea-sorrow.
Here in this island we arriv'd;
(Act 1, Scene 2)

_____

_____

_____

_____

The Tempest

Ariel
Full fathom five thy father lies,
    Of his bones are coral made.
Those are pearls that were his eyes.
    Nothing of him that doth fade,
but doth suffer a sea-change
Into something rich and strange.
Sea-nymphs hourly ring his knell:
               Ding-dong.

(Act 1, Scene 2)

Draw a stormy sea with a sinking ship.

The Tempest

Miranda
O, I have suffered
With those that I saw suffer.
(Act 1, Scene 2)

_____

_____

_____

_____

Prospero
My library was dukedom large enough.
(Act 1, Scene 2)

_____

_____

_____

_____

Prospero
Hast thou, spirit,
Perform'd to point the tempest that I bade thee?
(Act 1, Scene 2)

_____

_____

_____

_____

The Tempest

Ariel
The king's son, Ferdinand,
With hair up-staring—then like reeds, not hair—

_____

_____

_____

_____

Was the first man that leaped; cried, "Hell is empty,
And all the devils are here."
(Act 1, Scene 2)

_____

_____

_____

_____

Caliban
For I am all the subjects that you have,
Which first was mine own king.
(Act 1, Scene 2)

_____

_____

_____

_____

William Shakespeare

The Tempest

Trinculo
Misery acquaints a man with strange bedfellows.
(Act 2, Scene 2)

_____

_____

_____

_____

Caliban
Hast thou not dropped from heaven?
(Act 2, Scene 2)

_____

_____

_____

_____

Stephano
Out o' the moon, I do assure thee: I was the
man i' the moon when time was.
(Act 2, Scene 2)

_____

_____

_____

_____

The Tempest

Ferdinand
I, Beyond all limit of what else i'the world,
Do love, prize, honour you.
(Act 3, Scene 1)

_____

_____

_____

_____

Miranda
I am your wife, if you will marry me:
If not, I'll die your maid: to be your fellow

_____

_____

_____

_____

You may deny me, but I'll be your servant,
Whether you will or no.
(Act 3, Scene 1)

_____

_____

_____

_____

The Tempest

Prospero
Our revels now are ended. These our actors,
As I foretold you, were all spirits and
Are melted into air, into thin air;

And, like the baseless fabric of this vision,
The cloud-capp'd towers, the gorgeous palaces,
The solemn temples, the great globe itself,
Yea, all which it inherit, shall dissolve,

And, like this insubstantial pageant faded,
Leave not a rack behind. We are such stuff
As dreams are made on: and our little life
Is rounded with a sleep.
(Act 4, Scene 1)

The Tempest

Prospero
But this rough magic
I here abjure; and, when I have requir'd
Some heavenly music, which even now I do,

_____

_____

_____

_____

To work mine end upon their senses, that
This airy charm is for, I'll break my staff,
Bury it certain fathoms in the earth,

_____

_____

_____

_____

And, deeper than did ever plummet sound,
I'll drown my book.
(Act 5, Scene 1)

_____

_____

_____

_____

The Tempest

Ariel

Where the bee sucks, there suck I:
In a cowslip's bell I lie:
There I couch when owls do cry.
On the bat's back I do fly
After summer merrily.
Merrily, merrily, shall I live now
Under the blossom that hangs on the bough.
(Act 5, Scene 1)

Draw Ariel, the sprite.

The Tempest

Prospero
Why, that's my dainty Ariel! I shall miss thee;
But yet thou shalt have freedom.
(Act 5, Scene 1)

_____

_____

_____

_____

Miranda
O, wonder!
How many goodly creatures are there here!

_____

_____

_____

_____

How beauteous mankind is! O brave new world,
That has such people in't.
(Act 5, Scene 1)

_____

_____

_____

_____

The Tempest

Prospero
Now my charms are all o'erthrown,
And what strength I have's mine own:
Which is most faint: now, 'tis true,
I must be here confin'd by you,
Or sent to Naples. Let me not,
Since I have my dukedom got,
And pardon'd the deceiver, dwell
In this bare island, by your spell;
But release me from my bands,
With the help of your good hands.

Continued on next page.

Draw Prospero, "Now my charms are all o'erthrown..."

155

The Tempest

Continued from previous page.

Gentle breath of yours my sails
Must fill, or else my project fails,
Which was to please. Now I want
Spirits to enforce, art to enchant;
And my ending is despair,
Unless I be reliev'd by prayer;
Which pierces so, that it assaults
Mercy itself, and frees all faults.
As you from crimes would pardon'd be,
Let your indulgence set me free.
(Epilogue)

Draw an illustration for *The Tempest*.

156

The Tempest

TWELFTH NIGHT
OR
WHAT
YOV WILL

Twelfth Night

Orsino

If music be the food of love, play on;
Give me excess of it, that, surfeiting,
The appetite may sicken, and so die.
That strain again! it had a dying fall:
O, it came o'er my ear like the sweet sound
That breathes upon a bank of violets,
Stealing and giving odour! Enough; no more:
'T is not so sweet now as it was before.
(Act 1, Scene 1)

"If music be the food of love, play on..."

Twelfth Night

Viola
What country, friends, is this?
(Act 1, Scene 2)

_____

_____

_____

_____

Viola
Conceal me what I am, and be my aid
For such disguise as haply shall become
The form of my intent. I'll serve this duke
(Act 1, Scene 2)

_____

_____

_____

_____

Sir Andrew
But I am a great eater of beef and I believe that does harm to my wit.
(Act 1, Scene 3)

_____

_____

_____

_____

Twelfth Night

Viola
I'll do my best
To woo your lady: yet, a barful strife!
Whoe'er I woo, myself would be his wife.
(Act 1, Scene 4)

_____

_____

_____

_____

Feste
Many a good hanging prevents a bad marriage.
(Act 1, Scene 5)

_____

_____

_____

_____

Feste
Better a witty fool than a foolish wit.
(Act 1, Scene 5)

_____

_____

_____

_____

Twelfth Night

Viola
Make me a willow cabin at your gate,
And call upon my soul within the house.
(Act 1, Scene 5)

_____

_____

_____

Olivia
How now?
Even so quickly may one catch the plague?
(Act 1, Scene 5)

_____

_____

_____

Viola
O time! thou must untangle this, not I;
It is too hard a knot for me to untie.
(Act 2, Scene 2)

_____

_____

_____

Twelfth Night

Sir Toby
Dost thou think, because thou art virtuous, there shall be no more cakes and ale?
(Act 2, Scene 3)

_____

_____

_____

_____

Sir Andrew
I was adored once too.
(Act 2, Scene 3)

_____

_____

_____

_____

Duke
O, fellow, come, the song we had last night.
(Act 2, Scene 4)

_____

_____

_____

_____

Twelfth Night

Clown
    Come away, come away, death,
And in sad cypress let me be laid;
    Fly away, fly away, breath;
I am slain by a fair cruel maid.
My shroud of white, stuck all with yew,
      O, prepare it!
My part of death, no one so true
    Did share it.

Continued on next page.

Draw the clown.

Twelfth Night

Continued from previous page.

Not a flower, not a flower sweet,
On my black coffin let there be strown:
Not a friend, not a friend greet
My poor corpse, where my bones shall be thrown:
A thousand thousand sighs to save,
Lay me, O, where
Sad true lover never find my grave,
To weep there!

Twelfth Night

Viola
She pined in thought,
And with a green and yellow melancholy

She sat like patience on a monument,
Smiling at grief.
(Act 2, Scene 4)

Malvolio
In my stars I am above thee; but be not afraid of greatness: some are born great,
  some achieve greatness and some have greatness thrust upon 'em.
(Act 2, Scene 5)

Twelfth Night

Olivia
Love sought is good, but given unsought is better.
(Act 3, Scene 1)

_____

_____

_____

_____

Olivia
Why, this is very midsummer madness.
(Act 3, Scene 4)

_____

_____

_____

_____

Feste
Foolery, sir, does walk about the orb like the sun, it shines every where.
(Act 3, Scene 1)

_____

_____

_____

_____

Twelfth Night

Antonio
Let me speak a little. This youth that you see here
I snatch'd one half out of the jaws of death.
(Act 3, Scene 4)

_____

_____

_____

_____

Fabian
If this were played upon a stage now, I could condemn it as an improbable fiction.
(Act 3, Scene 4)

_____

_____

_____

_____

Viola
Prove true, imagination, O, prove true,
That I, dear brother, be now ta'en for you!
(Act 3, Scene 4)

_____

_____

_____

_____

Twelfth Night

Orsino
One face, one voice, one habit, and two persons,
A natural perspective, that is and is not!
(Act 5, Scene 1)

_____

_____

_____

_____

Feste
And thus the whirligig of time brings in his revenges.
(Act 5, Scene 1)

_____

_____

_____

_____

Malvolio
I'll be revenged on the whole pack of you.
(Act 5, Scene 1)

_____

_____

_____

_____

Twelfth Night

Draw Duke Orsino.

Orsino
Pursue him, and entreat him to a peace:
He hath not told us of the captain yet:
When that is known and golden time convents,
A solemn combination shall be made
Of our dear souls. Meantime, sweet sister,
We will not part from hence. Cesario, come;
For so you shall be, while you are a man;
But when in other habits you are seen,
Orsino's mistress and his fancy's queen.
(Act 5, Scene 1)

Twelfth Night

Clown, singing

When that I was and a little tiny boy,
  With hey, ho, the wind and the rain,
A foolish thing was but a toy,
  For the rain it raineth every day.

But when I came to man's estate,
  With hey, ho, the wind and the rain,
'Gainst knaves and thieves men shut their gate,
  For the rain it raineth every day.

Continued on next page.

Draw a storm or illustrate the poem how you wish.

Twelfth Night

But when I came, alas! to wive,
  With hey, ho, the wind and the rain,
By swaggering could I never thrive,
  For the rain it raineth every day.

But when I came unto my beds,
  With hey, ho, the wind and the rain,
With toss-pots still had drunken head,
  For the rain it raineth every day.

A great while ago the world begun,
  With hey, ho, the wind and the rain,
But that's all one, our play is done,
  And we'll strive to please you every day.
(Act 5, Scene 1)

Two Gentlemen of Verona

Proteus
That's a deep story of a deeper love,
For he was more than over shoes in love.
(Act 1, Scene 1)

_____

_____

_____

_____

Valentine
I have loved her ever since I saw her, and still I see her beautiful.
Speed
If you love her, you cannot see her.

_____

_____

_____

_____

Valentine
Why?
Speed
Because love is blind.
(Act 1, Scene 1)

_____

_____

_____

_____

Two Gentlemen of Verona

Lucetta
I have no other, but a woman's reason:
I think him so, because I think him so.
(Act 1, Scene 2)

Julia
They do not love, that do not show their love.
(Act 1, Scene 2)

Julia
You—minion—are too saucy.
(Act 1, Scene 2)

Two Gentlemen of Verona

Julia
O hateful hands, to tear such loving words;
Injurious wasps, to feed on such sweet honey,

_____

_____

_____

_____

And kill the bees that yield it with your stings;
I'll kiss each several paper, for amends.
(Act 1, Scene 2)

_____

_____

_____

_____

Proteus
Sweet love! sweet lines' sweet life'
Here is her hand, the agent of her heart;
Here is her oath for love, her honour's pawn.
(Act 1, Scene 3)

_____

_____

_____

_____

Two Gentlemen of Verona

Proteus
O, how this spring of love resembleth
The uncertain glory of an April day,
Which now shows all the beauty of the sun,
And by and by a cloud takes all away.
(Act 1, Scene 3)

What would the glory of an April day look like?

Two Gentlemen of Verona

Julia
I'll be as patient as a gentle stream,
And make a pastime of each weary step,
Till the last step have brought me to my love,
And there I'll rest, as after much turmoil,
A blessed soul doth in Elysium.
(Act 2, Scene 7)

Draw Julia.

Two Gentlemen of Verona

Valentine
That man that hath a tongue, I say, is no man,
If with his tongue he cannot win a woman.
(Act 3, Scene 1)

_____

_____

_____

_____

Duke
Love is like a child
That longs for every thing that he can come by.
(Act 3, Scene 1)

_____

_____

_____

_____

Valentine
What light is light, if Silvia be not seen?
What joy is joy, if Silvia be not by?
(Act 3, Scene 1)

_____

_____

_____

_____

Two Gentlemen of Verona

Julia
She dreams on him that has forgot her love—
You dote on her that cares not for your love...

_____

_____

_____

_____

'Tis pity love should be so contrary:
And thinking on it makes me cry, 'alas!'
(Act 4, Scene 4)

_____

_____

_____

_____

Proteus
O heaven, were man
But constant, he were perfect.
(Act 5, Scene 4)

_____

_____

_____

_____

Two Gentlemen of Verona

Duke
I think the boy hath grace in him: he blushes.

Valentine
I warrant you, my lord, more grace than boy.

Duke
What mean you by that saying?

Valentine
Please you, I'll tell you as we pass along,
That you will wonder what hath fortuned.

Continued on next page.

184

Two Gentlemen of Verona

Valentine
Come, Proteus; 'tis your penance, but to hear
The story of your loves discovered:
That done, our day of marriage shall be yours;
One feast, one house, one mutual happiness.
(Act 5, Scene 4)

Draw Valentine.

Two Gentlemen of Verona

The Winter's Tale

Camillo
You pay a great deal too dear for what's given freely.
(Act 1, Scene 1)

Hermione
Cram's with praise, and make's
As fat as tame things: one good deed, dying tongueless,
Slaughters a thousand waiting upon that.

Our praises are our wages: you may ride's
With one soft kiss a thousand furlongs ere
With spur we heat an acre.
(Act 1, Scene 2)

The Winter's Tale

Polixenes
What we changed
Was innocence for innocence; We knew not

_____

_____

_____

_____

The doctrine of ill-doing, nor dream'd
That any did.
(Act 1, Scene 2)

_____

_____

_____

_____

Camillo
Be plainer with me; let me know my trespass
By its own visage; if I then deny it,
'Tis none of mine.
(Act 1, Scene 2)

_____

_____

_____

_____

The Winter's Tale

Leontes
Is this nothing?
Why, then the world and all that's in't is nothing;

The covering sky is nothing; Bohemia nothing;
My wife is nothing; nor nothing have these nothings,
If this be nothing.
(Act 1, Scene 2)

Paulina
The silence often of pure innocence
Persuades when speaking fails.
(Act 2, Scene 2)

The Winter's Tale

Hermione
It shall scarce boot me
To say 'not guilty': mine integrity
Being counted falsehood, shall, as I express it,
Be so received. But thus: if powers divine
Behold our human actions, as they do,
I doubt not then but innocence shall make
False accusation blush and tyranny
Tremble at patience.
(Act 3, Scene 2)

The Winter's Tale

Leontes
Apollo's angry; and the heavens themselves
Do strike at my injustice.
(Act 3, Scene 2)

_____

_____

_____

_____

Paulina
What's gone and what's past help
Should be past grief.
(Act 3, Scene 2)

_____

_____

_____

_____

Leontes
Come and lead me
Unto these sorrows.
(Act 3, Scene 2)

_____

_____

_____

_____

The Winter's Tale

Shepherd
Heavy matters! heavy matters! but look thee here, boy. Now bless thyself: thou
  mettest with things dying, I with things newborn.

Here's a sight for thee: look thee; a bearing-cloth for a squire's child! Look thee here;
  take up, take up, boy; open't.

So, let's see: it was told me I should be rich by the fairies: this is some changeling:
Open't. What's within, boy?
(Act 3, Scene 3)

The Winter's Tale

Time (Chorus)

I, that please some, try all, both joy and terror,
Of good and bad, that make and unfold error,
Now take upon me, in the name of Time,
To use my wings. Impute it not a crime
To me or my swift passage, that I slide
O'er sixteen years and leave the growth untried
Of that wide gap, since it is in my power
To o'erthrow law and in one self-born hour
To plant and o'erwhelm custom.

Continued on next page.

How would you illustrate Time?
Maybe with an hourglass?

194

The Winter's Tale

Continued from previous page.

Let me pass
The same I am, ere ancient'st order was
Or what is now received: I witness to
The times that brought them in; so shall I do
To the freshest things now reigning and make stale
The glistering of this present, as my tale
Now seems to it.
(Act 4, Scene 1)

The Winter's Tale

Polixenes
Say there be;
Yet nature is made better by no mean,
But nature makes that mean: so, over that art

_____

_____

_____

_____

Which you say adds to nature, is an art
That nature makes.
(Act 4, Scene 3)

_____

_____

_____

_____

Autolycus
Ha, ha! What a fool Honesty is!
(Act 4, Scene 4)

_____

_____

_____

_____

The Winter's Tale

Autolycus
Though I am not naturally honest, I am so sometimes by chance.
(Act 4, Scene 4)

_____

_____

_____

Leontes
I am asham'd. Does not the stone rebuke me
For being more stone than it?
(Act 5, Scene 3)

_____

_____

_____

_____

Leontes
If this be magic, let it be an art
Lawful as eating.
(Act 5, Scene 3)

_____

_____

_____

_____

Leontes thinks he is seeing a sculpture of his wife Hermoine, when in fact, it is Hermoine herself, posing as a sculpture. Draw Hermoine looking like a Greek sculpture.

The Winter's Tale

Penmanship Practice Pages

Penmanship Practice Pages
Traditional Manuscript

Aa Bb Cc Dd Ee Ff Gg Hh Ii Jj Kk Ll Mm

Nn Oo Pp Qq Rr Ss Tt Uu Vv Ww Xx Yy Zz

A B C D E F G H I J K L M

N O P Q R S T U V W X Y Z

a b c d e f g h i j k l m

n o p q r s t u v w x y z

Virtue is bold, and goodness
never fearful.

Penmanship Practice Pages

Traditional Manuscript

Aa Bb Cc Dd Ee Ff Gg Hh Ii Jj Kk Ll Mm

Nn Oo Pp Qq Rr Ss Tt Uu Vv Ww Xx Yy Zz

A B C D E F G H I J K L M

N O P Q R S T U V W X Y Z

a b c d e f g h i j k l m

n o p q r s t u v w x y z

Virtue is bold, and goodness
never fearful.

William Shakespeare

Penmanship Practice Pages

Traditional Cursive

Aa Bb Cc Dd Ee Ff Gg Hh Ii Jj Kk Ll Mm

Nn Oo Pp Qq Rr Ss Tt Uu Vv Ww Xx Yy Zz

A B C D E F G H I J K L M

N O P Q R S T U V W X Y Z

a b c d e f g h i j k l m

n o p q r s t u v w x y z

Virtue is bold, and goodness never fearful.

Penmanship Practice Pages

Traditional Cursive

Aa Bb Cc Dd Ee Ff Gg Hh Ii Jj Kk Ll Mm

Nn Oo Pp Qq Rr Ss Tt Uu Vv Ww Xx Yy Zz

A B C D E F G H I J K L M

N O P Q R S T U V W X Y Z

a b c d e f g h i j k l m

n o p q r s t u v w x y z

Virtue is bold, and goodness never fearful.

William Shakespeare